Crochet
Hat Patterns

LEARN TO EASILY GIVE LIFE TO GORGEOUS CROCHET BEANIES, CAPS, AND HATS WITH THIS CROCHET GUIDE FOR BEGINNERS. | INCLUDING 15 STEP-BY-STEP CROCHET HAT PATTERNS

TABLE OF
CONTENTS

INTRODUCTION

The popularity of crocheting as a hobby is rising for many different reasons. Making your own clothes, toys, and household items is not only a great way to express your individuality, but it is also a great way to unwind, have fun, and strengthen relationships with loved ones if you decide to work on a project together. Taking on an Afghan project is a lot of fun, whether alone or in a group.

It is the goal of this tutorial to provide you with the information you need to crochet an Afghan in a day or less. Honestly, how else could you possibly fill your time? Even if you're just starting off, you'll have access to all the information you need within the following chapters, which include comprehensive guides to all the different stitches, techniques, and other essentials. The detailed instructions will guarantee that you won't get lost in the Afghan crochet pattern's instructions.

Crochet, which literally translates to 'hook' in French, is the art of making cloth out of yarn, thread, or other strands of material with the aid of a crochet hook. Metals, wood, or plastics can all be used to create these hooks. Like knitting, crocheting involves dragging loops of material through other loops. However, unlike knitting, only one stitch at a time is active in crochet, and the hook is used instead of knitting needles. This allows for a greater variety of stitches and the creation of really one-of-a-kind items. Crocheting is simpler to learn than other needle arts since it requires just one main tool. However, this freedom from additional equipment also allows for greater design freedom.

To begin, hold your crochet hook like you would a pencil by placing your thumb and index finger in the small depression in the center of the hook, also known as a finger hold. Slip your third finger up toward the hook's tip for simplicity and power. The hook will point in your general direction, but it won't be completely horizontal or vertical.

In crochet, there are many different stitches to learn, but for beginners, it's best to stick to the basics and work on simple chain stitches. By threading this loop through a second, similar loop, you'll create an interlocking oval symbol. Single crochet is a shorter cross than double crochet and is hence called a 'squat cross.' There is a bar in the center of the post in the double crochet symbol. The remaining symbols are also lined up in the same fashion. Puffs-out stitches may use a symbol that looks close to the short stitch, but this is not guaranteed.

Let's get started.

CHAPTER 1:
WHY DO CROCHETING?

Crochet is a wonderful craft, and once you master the basic stitches and techniques, the sky's the limit in terms of the patterns you can create! The more you practice, the easier it will be to create patterns of any complexity. Learning the many crochet stitches and techniques can be challenging at first, but with time and practice, you'll soon become an expert. The following are some suggestions that can make crocheting simpler for novices, allowing you to complete projects while doing other things like watching TV, driving, or cooking.

Many people around the world have mastered the art of crocheting. This is a result of the many benefits that come with it. Different people will, however, crochet for different reasons. There are many people out there who may be wondering why people crochet. They do not see enough reason why they should spend their free time crocheting. Most times, they lack the motivation to start crocheting, so it would be great to highlight a few reasons for crocheting.

It Brings a Great Sense of Accomplishment

There is no better feeling than seeing people wear or cover themselves with items that you crocheted yourself. It makes you feel great about the time you spent crocheting the items. It isn't a waste of time as you can see them enjoy the fruits of your labor. That feeling is so fulfilling that you will want to keep crocheting. You will also keep on discovering new patterns and after implementing the skill, there will be a great sense of fulfillment.

It Enables You to Have an Alert Mind

People grow older each day. Crocheting offers a lasting solution to people who would want to remain alert as well as stimulated. Someone has to remain alert, especially when working on a new pattern. Isn't it, therefore, important to engage our minds with crocheting?

It Is a Stress Reliever

Crocheting has been tried and proven to be one of the activities that help people to relieve stress. This is because as you crochet, you can forget all the challenges you may be going through. All your concentration is on pattern making so all your mind is occupied. While crocheting, everything in your mind evaporates which helps a lot in relaxing your mind. Whenever someone needs to learn a new crocheting skill, they have to go through different books, sites, and also apps that normally engage them mindfully. One forgets everything they are going through since they are curious to learn a new skill.

It Keeps You Busy

Whenever someone is crocheting, their mind is fully engaged. This means that they are busy and hence will not be thinking about anything else. Being busy is beneficial in that you won't be idling around without doing any meaningful thing. For most people, crocheting is a hobby, so they use their free time doing it.

Enhancing One's Creativity

We learn a new trick every day. Through crocheting, you can perfect your skills by designing new patterns. They can creatively mix different color schemes to develop beautiful patterns that make the crochets more appealing. It is through Crocheting that you can experience a comforting effect from the great textures created through repeated movements using yarns of different colors.

Health Benefit

Apart from relieving stress, crocheting is of great benefit to people suffering from arthritis. This is because as someone works through various stitches, the fingers remain nimble hence reducing the risks of arthritis. People who get Alzheimer's attacks are also advised to consider engaging in crocheting. This is because they are able to reduce the attacks by a great percentage. Whenever they engage in learning a new skill, they get to preserve some of the memories they have made in the past.

Technical Abbreviations

- Alt: Alternate.
- Beg: Means beginning, as the beginning of the row.
- Bp: Means 'back post' like rather than working through the loops, you are working the stitch around the post. You typically pair it with the abbreviation of the stitch you are using. For example, bpdc stands for back post double crochet, whereas bpsc stands for back post single crochet.
- BL: Refers to the 'back loop' crochet. It might also be seen as BLO 'back loop only.' Occasionally BL can also be used to refer to bobbles or blocks, specific to the pattern using it. For this information, check the stitch list of the pattern that is usually found at the beginning of the pattern.
- BO: Bobble.
- Cl: Cluster. Your pattern should specify the type of cluster being used, as there are many different types of clusters. For instance, 3 tr cluster refers to a cluster of 3 treble crochet stitches.
- Ch(s): Chain(s). This is one of the most common abbreviations you will see since almost all crochet patterns start with chains. Most patterns also include chains throughout the design.
- Dtr: Double treble crochet.
- Dec: Decrease. It's a technique used for shaping in crochet.
- Dc: Double crochet. It's one of the most common basic crocheting stitches.
- Incl: Inclusive/including/include.
- Inc: Increase. It's another technique used in shaping like dec (decreasing) is used.
- Hdc or half dc: Half double crochet. It's a basic crochet stitch in between double

crochet and single crochet in height.

- Fp: Front post, as compared to 'back post' explained above.
- FL: Front loop. It is also abbreviated as FLO (front loop only) in contrast to BL/BLO as earlier mentioned.
- Oz: Ounce(s). It's likely to be seen in the part of the patterns of crocheting, explaining how much yarn is required or on yarn labels. It may also be measured in other ways, such as yards (yd), meters (m), or grams (g).
- Pm: Place marker.
- Pc: Popcorn. A textured crochet stitch that is similar to bobbles and clusters. Patterns that use these types of stitches normally explain how the designer wants to make the stitch at the beginning of the pattern, where the crochet abbreviation preferred by the designer will also be seen.
- Rem: Remaining.
- RS: Right side. Crochet has both a right side and a wrong side when working in rows.
- Round (s): Round(s). They are used for counting when working in a round or otherwise working in circles (in contrast to working in rows).
- Rev: Reverse. It is typically used together with other abbreviations such as rev sc, which means reverse single crochet stitch.
- Rep: Repeat. It is frequently placed together with symbols that show the part of the pattern that is going to be repeated. Examples:
  - ✓ []: The pattern specifies the times to repeat a series of instructions given inside the brackets
  - ✓ (): The pattern specifies the times to repeat a series of instructions given inside the parentheses
  - ✓ *: The pattern specifies the times to repeat a series of instructions given between asterisks or following an asterisk
- St(s): Stitch(es).
- Sp(s): Space (s).
- Sl st: slip stitch. It's the method used in joining rounds when crocheting, as well as a stitch that is used on its own.
- Sk: Skip. For instance, you can skip the next chain and work into the one following, which will be indicated by the term sk ch (skip chain).
- Sc: Single crochet. It is one of the most basic and frequently used crochet stitches.

- Tr: Triple crochet/treble crochet. It's another basic crochet stitch.
- Tr: Triple treble crochet. Another tall crochet stitch is even taller than the dtr described earlier.
- Tog: Together. It is sometimes used to replace 'decrease' where it can be written as 'sc2tog' to mean a decrease in a single crochet stitch.
- WS: Wrong side. It's the opposite of the right side (rs) as earlier described.
- WIP: Work in progress.
- Yoh: Yarn over hook.
- YO: Yarn over. A step used in making most crochet stitches. It's typically not seen in crochet patterns but is often seen in crochet stitch tutorials.

CHAPTER 2:
HOW TO CHOOSE A CROCHET PATTERN

Mussel Pattern

For this pattern, three or more stitches are crocheted into the same puncture site, forming a triangle that looks like a small shell. On the left and right of the shell, a few stitches are often passed to compensate for the increased stitches of the shells, which turns one stitch into at least three. Shells look best if you crochet them out of chopsticks or double sticks.

In order to crochet a mussel out of three sticks, work first, on where the stitch is to be placed, first a stick, to be able to work. Then in the same puncture, place two more sticks. To complete the pattern and the number of stitches in the row, it can sometimes be necessary to crochet half-shells at the beginning and end of the row. To do this, at the beginning of each turn, work two sticks into the corresponding puncture site. At the end of the row, place two sticks in the last stitch.

Tuft Stitches

Tufts are basically nothing but inverted shells. They consist of several stitched-together stitches; these can be fixed stitches but also double or multiple sticks. Not only do they provide a decorative pattern, but they are also often used to remove one or more stitches in a row.

The base of this tuft is spread over several stitches while their heads are gathered in a stitch. To do this, do not crochet the stitches you want to gather at first to pull the thread in one go through all loops on the needle in the last step. How to do it exactly shows the following instructions for a tuft of three sticks.

Work the first stick as usual until there are only two loops on the needle. Do the same with the second stick so that you have a total of three loops on the needle.

The third stick is also crocheted up to and including the penultimate step. There are four loops on the needle. Now, get the thread.

To complete the tufting, pull the thread through all four loops on the needle.

Burl

Knob stitches are very distinctive and give the crochet a beautiful plastic structure. It is a group of several rods or multiple rods, which are worked in the same puncture site and then blended together, making it a combination of shell and tufts. Pimples are worked in the back row. The following shows how to crochet a knot stitch out of five sticks.

Crochet the first stick at the point where you want to create the knit stitch until you have only two loops on the needle.

Follow the same procedure for the following four rods working in the same puncture site.

Now, there should be a total of six loops on the crochet hook.

In the last step, pick up the thread and pull it in one go through all the loops on the needle. It is advisable to secure the knit stitch with a chain stitch (take the thread and pull it once again through the stitch on the needle) so that the stitches remain firmly together at the top and the knobby effect maintains the desired plasticity.

Colorful Pimples

It looks happy when you work the pimples in different colors. In addition, you can meaningfully use small yarn remnants in this way.

To crochet a colored nub, work the last solid stitch in front of the nub in the base color until there are still two loops on the needle to finish the stitch with the yarn for the nub. Then crochet the nub as described in the new color. Use the chain stitch to secure the knob; work again in the basic color, with which you then continue crocheting until the next knob.

Flat Nubs

Flat knobs are made of half-sticks and are slightly less plastic than knobs or the popcorn stitches described below. They are often used to crochet baby clothes and cuddly blankets. They are crocheted according to the same principle as the pimples. You mustn't work too hard. The following example illustrates how to crochet a flat knot of three half rods in one go through all the loops on the needle. It is advisable to secure the knit stitch with a chain stitch (take the thread and pull it once again through the stitch on the needle) so that the stitches remain firmly together at the top, and the knobby effect maintains the desired plasticity.

First, thread the yarn around the needle, then insert it into the loop into which the flat knot should be placed. Get the thread.

Repeat this step twice so that there are finally seven loops on the crochet hook. Then you pick the thread and pull it in one go through all the loops.

Finally, secure the flat knot with a warp stitch by retrieving the thread and pulling it through the loop on the crochet hook.

Popcorn Stitches

For a popcorn mesh, one works—as well as the knobs or flat knobs—a whole group of stitches in a puncture site. The stitches are not taken off together but individually terminated and bundled in a further step. They create plastic accents in even patterns and can be crocheted from fine yarn, as well as from thicker wool qualities.

Crochet a group of five rods in a single injection site when you wanted to crochet a shell. Then slightly lengthen the working loop on the needle by pulling lightly. Now, pull the needle out of the working loop in order to put it into the debarking element (i.e., the mesh V) of the first stick.

Then, pick up the working loop and pull it through the second loop on the needle (the debittering stick of the first stick). Secure the stitch with a chain stitch. Pull the thread through the loop again.

Filet or Net Pattern

For this effective but, in principle, quite simple pattern, you crochet from bars and air meshes a grid. You can combine filled and empty boxes in such a way that geometric or floral motifs are created. A simple net pattern without 'fillings' can be crocheted very fast. For example, it is good for light scarves and bandages, and if you can handle it with sturdy material works, you would have crocheted, in no time, a shopping net. If you work alternately filled and empty boxes, you can pull a cord through the stitches to close about a bag.

Crochet a chain of meshes first. The number of stitches for your basic chain must be divisible by two. In addition, crochet six more pieces of air.

Now, for the first box, insert into the sixth stitch of the chain of stitches as seen from the needle and work a chopstick.

Crochet an airlock again. For the subsequent chopsticks, pass over a stitch in the sling chain. Then, crochet one more air mesh and the next chopstick into the next, but one mesh of the basic chain work. So, continue until the end of the series.

Start the next row with three first-streaks and one streak with the next-stick link.

Now, work a chopstick into the scraping member of the penultimate stick of the previous row, crochet a loop of air, pass one stitch of the previous row, and work another stick into the corresponding chopsticks of the previous row. The last stitch of the row works in the third link of the chain of meshes counted from below.

To crochet a filled box, do not join the sticks with an airlock, but crochet between the base stick's other sticks around the air mesh of the previous row. To do this, just stick in the empty box to get the thread.

If the box of the previous row is also filled, work the 'stuffing stick' into the scraping member of the pre-row filler.

Grid Pattern

A likewise light and transparent pattern is the grid pattern, which is crocheted from air mesh and solid or warp stitches. Experimental minds vary the length of the air-chain chains to work an uneven lattice structure.

Normally, the arcs are one-third longer than the basic piece of the previous series. The arcs in the following instructions are five air mesh long, the base three chains.

Work an air chain. The number of stitches should be divisible by four. For this crochet, add two air meshes.

Now, anchor the first bow by crocheting it into the sixth stitch of the base with a slit stitch or a sturdy stitch. Then crochet five loops of air, pass three meshes in the basic loop and anchor the bow in the fourth loop of the air.

The last bow of the row is attached to the last loop of the base chain.

Now, crochet five air stitches and then a single crochet stitch into the bow, then another five stitches, and then a single crochet stitch into the next bow. The last bow is anchored in the third spiral of the first row.

Start the next series again with five air stitches, fasten them with a sturdy stitch in the first loop of air mesh, and work in the grid pattern to the end of the row.

The last tight stitch back into the third spiral air mesh of the front row work. Continue working until the desired height is reached.

Crochet Subjects Around an Air-Mesh Bow

In crochet instructions for flowers, for example, you can often read the instruction that a group of stitches, often chopsticks, should be worked into an air-mesh arch. For this, you do not sting into the mesh links of the chain but into the bow so that the chain of mesh is crocheted.

Types of Yarn

Wool Yarn

Wool yarn is a great choice if you are a beginner. You will find that it is flexible and very forgiving. If you make a mistake using wool, it is very easy to unravel that portion of your project with the mistake and re-crochet it. However, you may have difficulty wearing wool if you or a family member is allergic to wool. In that case, you should choose another type of yarn. Also, the wool yarn is more expensive than other types of yarn, which may be a factor for you and your project.

Cotton Yarn

Cotton yarn is less forgiving than wool yarn. It has less given to it and will not stretch. This makes it slightly harder to crochet with, especially if you are a beginner. However, it is a lighter yarn to work with, so if you do not like the heat or warmth of crocheting a project made of wool, you should consider using cotton yarn.

Acrylic Yarn

Wool and cotton yarn are both natural fibers. Acrylic yarn is human-made. It is usually the least expensive option for crafters and comes in a wide variety of colors and types. It is a good choice for beginners, however, if you are looking to create a family heirloom, you may wish to choose a natural fiber.

Animal Fibers

Animal fibers used to create yarn include wool, alpaca, mohair, cashmere, angora, and silk. Wool and alpaca are very similar in feel and both give you a nice spongy and warm fabric. Mohair comes from goats and is usually dyed with very vivid colors. Coarse mohair comes from older animals while softer mohair comes from young animals. Cashmere and angora are very luxurious and can be a bit pricey. Cashmere is taken from the underbelly of a specific breed of goat. Angora comes from the fur of the Angora rabbit.

Plant Fibers

The plant fibers used to create yarn include cotton, bamboo, hemp, and linen. Cotton yarn is perfect for kitchen projects and summer garments. It is strong, absorbs water, and is easy to care for with machine washing and drying. Bamboo is a bit finer and has more shine than cotton and can be used for many projects. Bamboo yarn will give you a very pretty stitch definition and is perfect for delicate projects. Hemp is also another sturdy plant-based yarn, and linen is great for warm-weather garments since it breathes and wicks away moisture.

Yarn Selection

The following step is the selection of the yarn for the project. The thickness and size of your project, as well as your knitting skills, will help you determine the right type of yarn for crocheting. If you are a beginner and trying crocheting for the first time, select a yarn that has a light color (this will help you see the stitches correctly), smooth texture, and medium (worsted) weight.

You will need 3 to 4 yarns to make a receiving blanket or a lap blanket. Now keep that count and estimate the skeins of yarn you will need for larger blankets.

If you are not sure about the number of skeins you will be needing for a particular project, it is a wise idea to keep a few extra to avoid your crocheting from delaying (don't forget you just have a day to complete your project).

Here is an important tip: If you are getting your yarn skeins from a dye lot, be very careful in choosing the same color for each skein. The trick is to check the dye lot number printed on the label. This will help you pick up the same color yarn. Otherwise, your skeins might be slightly different in color and will be visible when the project is completed.

Since crocheting is impossible without yarn, make sure you pay extra attention to this one. The overall quality and beauty of your finished product will depend on the quality and colors of the yarn you choose. So, make your choice wisely.

Read the label of the yarn to grasp the data found therein. For knowing the weight, fiber quality, prescribed hook, care directions, and gauge, a yarn label is your best source.

Buy more of the same dye lot than you need if the yarn you select has a dye lot number. Today, not all yarns have dye loads, but if they do, it's a smart idea to have more yarn than you use so that as you add new yarn, you don't run out, and the color changes.

As long as they are of the same weight and fiber material, you can replace yarn labels. For example, if Vanna's Option is called for by the pattern, but your fiber material. For instance, if the pattern needs Vanna's Preference, but you only have Red Heart, just make sure the weights of the yarns are the same. This will guarantee that, as you intend it to, the idea works out.

Secure the pricey wool for today. If you see the yarn that you like, go ahead and buy it and save it for later. Stick to mid-range yarns, which are straightforward to deal with and convenient to care for, for now.

Remember not to smoke around or when you're crocheting your yarn stash. Yarn takes up smells quickly because you don't want your project to smell like tobacco smoke while you're making a present. You should put it in a pillowcase, tie the pillowcase and wash it and dry it on the gentle machine if you get wool as a gift and it has an odor. It typically prevents cotton odors and leaves intact the yarn balls and skeins.

Understanding Patterns

Patterns today are written instructions, often wrought with abbreviations. Before, in the early days of crochet, patterns were the actual crocheted item of someone else. For example, a lady wanted to crochet a wrist cuff. A written pattern was not available. Instead, she had to get an actual wrist cuff and painstakingly count the stitches and copy them. Then came the scrapbooks. Fragments of crocheted work were sewn on pieces of paper and bound together like a scrapbook. Some had crocheted samples sewn onto larger fabrics, while some were simply kept in a box or bag. Crochet stitch samples were also made in long and narrow bands.

In 1824, the earliest crochet pattern was printed. The patterns were for making purses from silver and gold threads.

Early crochet reading materials from the 1800s were small. These may be small (4 inches by 6 inches) but they contain a treasure of crochet patterns for lace, cuffs, lace-like collars, insertions, caps (women's, men's, and children's), purses, and men's slippers. It also contained patterns for white crochet, which were for undergarment trimmings, mats, edgings, and insertions. The recommended materials such as cotton thread, hemp thread, spool yarn, and linen thread. Colorwork was done in chenille, wool, and silk yarns, with the occasional silver and gold threads.

The problem with these early patterns was their inaccuracy. For example, the pattern is for an 8-point star but would turn out to be with only 6 points. These crochet reading materials required the reader to rely more on the woodwork illustrations as a better guide.

Today, crochet patterns are more systematic, accurate, and organized. However, to the uninitiated, looking at a crochet pattern is a lot like looking at letters and numbers with no idea what they meant. Look for the meanings of the abbreviations, which are often printed at the bottom of the pattern. If not, research some of the unfamiliar abbreviations.

A crocheter needs to learn the abbreviations and symbols used in a crochet pattern. Without this knowledge, there will be a very limited number of patterns that a crocheter can work with, as most are written in the crochet language.

Here are a few things to remember when working with patterns:

- Patterns are either made in rounds or rows. The pattern will specify if using either or both.
- Patterns come with a difficulty rating. Crocheters should choose the level best suited to their abilities. That is, beginners should stick to patterns suited to their level while they are still familiarizing themselves with the terms and techniques. Move to higher difficulty levels after gaining enough experience and mastery of the required crochet skills.
- Always count the stitches made while working then after reaching the end of the row or round.
- Always check the gauge, especially if the project has to turn out the exact size and shape as indicated in the pattern.
- Learning to read crochet patterns requires practice and experience. Be patient and do not get this outraged.

How to Read a Crochet Pattern?

Crochet patterns would often only list the abbreviations and the number of stitches required for each row or round. Some patterns would also use abbreviations for other instructions such as when to turn or when to begin and end.

The simplest crochet pattern would look like this:

Row 1: Use a size E crochet hook, ch15, single crochet 2nd ch from hook, and for each ch, turn.

(14 single crochet)

This can look more like a foreign language to the uninitiated. This is still the simplest of crochet patterns. Translated, the line means:

Row 1: With a crochet hook size E, make 15 chain stitches. Starting on the 2nd stitch from the hook, make a single crochet stitch across the chain stitches. Then make a turning stitch. By the end of the row, there should be 14 single crochet stitches done.

Circle Patterns

Circles are also common in crochet. It starts with a center ring, which is the foundation of all rounds, as the foundation chain is to work in rows. The center ring is created either by making a ring from chain stitches or from in single chain stitch. The first method creates a hole in the middle of the circle crochet work. The second method has an inconspicuous middle.

Working With a Hole as a Center Ring

This is the most common way of making a center ring. A row of chain stitches is created and then looped off to make a ring. The hole in the middle is determined by how many chain stitches were made at the beginning. It also determines how many stitches can be made through the center ring. Avoid making the chain stitch too long because the resulting ring would be too large and unsteady.

Ch6 (make 6 chain stitches).

Place the crochet hook into the 1st chain stitch, the one farthest from the crochet hook, and follow to the slip knot. This will now form a ring.

Do 1 yarn over.

Through the chain stitch and the loop resting on the crochet hook, pull the yarn. This completes the center ring with a hole visible in the middle.

Working with a hole for a center is easy because the stitches are made by going through the center hole instead of into the actual chain stitches of the ring.

From the finished center ring above, make ch1 as a turning chain to be used for the single crochet of the first row.

Place the crochet hook through the center ring.

Make 1 yo. Pull the wrapped yarn through the hole (center ring).

Make another yo and pull it through the 2 loops resting in the crochet hook. This finishes 1 single crochet (single crochet).

Continue making single crochet through the center hole until it cannot fit anymore.

Working Into the Chain Stitch

This is another way of working in rounds. This is used when the pattern calls for a very small or barely noticeable center hole. Generally, you start with a slipknot and ch1, then add the number of chain stitches required for a turning chain. For example, make 1 chain stitch and then another 3 if using double crochet because the turning chains for dc are 3 chain stitches.

Ch1.

If using dc, make ch3.

Perform 1 yarn over and place the hook into the center of the 4th chain stitch from the hook. This is the 1st ch made and is located to the slipknot.

Make 1 double crochet into this chain stitch. Continue making dc on the other chain stitches.

To the uninitiated, a crochet pattern might look like it is written in a completely different language, and in a way; it is. Designers and crocheters use a language of abbreviations and conventions that are standardized, which makes it easy for anyone who understands this language to follow a pattern. The following is a breakdown of the most common ways information is relayed in a crochet pattern—and what it all means.

Materials

The materials are where the designer indicates everything the crocheter will need to complete the pattern. This usually includes the yarn, hook size, and any extra notions or items. Sometimes patterns include the brand names of yarn or other items, but sometimes they merely contain the type of item needed (Lion Brand Fishermen's Wool Yarn versus 100 percent worsted-weight yarn, for example). One important item to pay attention to in the materials is the amount of yarn needed; little is more frustrating than running out of yarn in the middle of a project!

Gauge

Gauge is a dreaded word to even experienced crocheters, but it does not have to be. Put simply, the gauge is the measurement of the number of crochet stitches and rows per inch of fabric. Why is this important? Because achieving the proper gauge ensures that the finished item will turn out the correct size. Ignore the gauge, and what is supposed to be a cropped, snug cardigan might become a housedress.

A pattern will indicate the gauge is either over 1 inch or 4 inches of stitches. For example, a gauge might read: '3 stitches and 4 rows over 1 inch in single crochet.' This means that if the crocheter works a fabric in single crochet, he or she should have 3 stitches and 4 rows in every inch when using the hook size indicated in the materials.

Before beginning a project, the crocheter checks that they are getting gauge by crocheting at least a 4-inch by 4-inch swatch in the pattern stitch (in the prior example, single crochet), then blocking it, then measuring it carefully. If the gauge matches that given, it is okay to start the project. If the gauge does not match, the crocheter needs to change either the hook size or the yarn until they get the gauge. This is necessary because small differences in gauge can equal big differences in a finished item: a row of 30 single crochet at 3 stitches per inch will be 10 inches long, whereas a row of 30 single crochet at 4 stitches per inch will only be 7.5 inches long—not an unimportant difference.

The crocheter should generally change the hook size before changing the yarn. If the gauge is smaller than that given (e.g., 2 stitches per inch instead of 3), the hook is too large. If the gauge is larger than that given (e.g., 4 stitches per inch instead of 3), the hook is too small. Row gauge is much more adaptable in crochet, but the crocheter should still aim to get the gauge of both.

Note that with some projects, the gauge is more important than with others. For items with a lot of shaping, including sweaters, mittens, socks, and hats, the gauge is critical. For items that are more 'one size fits all', a small difference in gauge might be okay—a scarf that is an inch wider than the designer intended is not necessarily the end of the world.

Abbreviations

The abbreviations part includes all of the abbreviations used in the pattern. Many times, this part includes instructions for working special stitches. If a crocheter does not understand some of the stitches used in the pattern, the abbreviations part is a good place to look for help. Many abbreviations are standardized, so as crocheters gain practice reading patterns, they learn to immediately recognize sc for single crochet, dc for double crochet, and so on.

Instructions

The instructions are the meat of the pattern, the place where the designer tells the crocheter what to do to make the item. For the most part, designers are explicit—'Chain 3, work 3 for turning chain, double crochet into the third chain from hook'—but a few common shortcuts are used as well, including:

- **Asterisks**: Asterisks are used to indicate repeats of patterns. A pattern might read: 'Chain 1, slip stitch into the second chain from hook, 3 single crochet, ch 2, 3 single crochet, repeat from * to * three times, chain 1, turn'. The stitches within the asterisks are repeated three times in the sequence they are given after the first time they are worked. So, in total, the asterisk part would be repeated four times.

- **Parentheses**: Parentheses are used to indicate repeats, often within asterisks. Changing the prior example, the crocheter might see: '...*3 single crochet, (ch 2, single crochet) twice, 3 single crochet*, repeat from * to * three times.' To work the directions inside the asterisks, the crocheter would work 3 single crochet, 2 chains, 1 single crochet, 2 chains, 1 single crochet, then 3 more single crochet.

Then the crocheter would repeat the instructions inside the asterisks the number of times called for. Many crochet patterns are also broken down into rows and rounds (for circular crochet). Pattern repeats are often made up of many rows or rounds, which the designer will indicate in the pattern.

CHAPTER 3:
BASIC CROCHET TECHNIQUES

We'll learn the simple crochet techniques you need to learn as a beginner in this portion. At the beginning of the row and in the middle of a row, the methods we'll discuss are crocheting in the ring, changing colors, how to join yarn when you run out, or the yarn splits, and more crochet techniques you can use to make your designs work easily and make your life a lot simpler.

Crocheting in the Round

This method can be used for several ventures, such as hats. Insert the hook through the first chain, yarn over, and pull the yarn through the chain and the loop on the hook after you have made your base chain. This is referred to as entering. I would strongly recommend that you apply to the joining chain a stitch marker. You've got a circle of stitches now. It will become very difficult to say where the round starts until you start going through your project.

You'll find your seam is going in a diagonal direction when you crochet in the round. This is natural, and the trends work exactly the way they work. This is especially true if, over the pattern, you have decreased or increased. It is necessary to count your stitches in the round while you crochet so that your project works out correctly.

Magic Ring

You end up with a tiny hole in the middle of the circle when you use a base chain and connect it with a slip stitch. Although this is completely appropriate for most tasks, there are certain occasions when you want to close the circle. This is where it's useful to know how to do a magic ring. I'll now confess that it takes some practice to master this technique. Until it actually clicked, I had to replay a video several times, and I can now do it without having to look it up.

Place the yarn on the palm of your hand and drape the yarn over your index finger. Wrap the yarn around your middle finger and index finger and catch the end of your little finger attached to the skein. Insert the hook on your index finger beneath the string and grab the thread. Draw it through the loop and once again take the thread and draw it on the hook through the loop. Continue to work around the circle with the starting stitches of the first round. Grab the loose tail of yarn after you've done the stitches and carefully draw it up before the stitches touch. The stitches should then be combined, and you'll have a solid circle of stitches to deal with.

Changing Colors

The use of various shades is one of crochet's fun things. Changing colors may seem like a challenge for a beginner but it's really simple. Simply work the last stitch before you have two loops on your hook, whether you have hit the end of a row and choose to swap colors. Pick up the new color and draw along the two loops with it. Switch the job around and do the chain stitches for the next row's first stitch and softly pull the old color and the snug new color. Leave the old hue with a six-inch tail so that you can weave it in.

You can use the very same strategy if you need to change the colors in the middle row. Work the last stitch of the old color, take the new color, and drag it along until you have two loops on your hook. Work a couple of the following stitches and then snugly pull the shades. Don't pull them too close, or you're going to make the fabric pucker. Leave a tail of six inches to weave in later on.

To take care of those annoying tails, you can use a few tricks so that in the end, you don't have a lot of them to weave in. Beneath the fresh threads, you can grab the tails of the thread. To do this, make sure your hook goes under both the new color and the tails of the old color and catch them before you hit the end of the tails in your stitches. Another strategy is to take the tails and thread them in and out of the previous row's stitches and then crochet them to make sure you put the hook under the tails. This is a really good way to lock your tails and when you're done, stop trying to weave in a lot of them.

Weaving in Tails

This is a work that few want to do, but to protect the tails of your wool, you have to do it. Using a tapestry or wool needle and stitching the tails into the stitches is the best way I have learned. Insert the needle and change the course nearly three times under the loops of the stitches. This really secures the wool ends, and they won't work out of the cloth their way.

How to Join Yarn

Perhaps you run out of thread while you're crocheting. So now, what are you doing? We will discuss two separate approaches for a smooth join in this segment so that you can carry on crocheting without having to frog back to the beginning of a row your job.

Spit Splicing

For animal fiber yarns, such as wool, alpaca, cashmere, and other types of animal fibers, the first approach can only be used. On plant and synthetic yarns, do not attempt to use this method because they do not naturally feel up. And yes, spit can be used by you. Your saliva contains enzymes that help break down the fabric fibers, and the yarn spontaneously fills and links itself when combined with the heat generated by the friction of rubbing the palms together.

Fry the ends of the old and new yarn first. Now lick your hands' palms and place the yarns with the ends overlapping on the side. Rub the palms firmly together until the yarns form one strand. To get the splice to stay, you can have to rub it a couple of times. You have one continuous yarn strand now, and you should keep crocheting.

Russian Join

You may use the Russian joining method for any form of yarn fiber. To execute this yarn-joining process, you will require a tapestry needle. For one of the threads of yarn, loop the needle and sew the yarn back into itself for a few inches. Move to the other piece of yarn and fasten the needle with string. Through the loop created by stitching the first yarn back on itself, bring the needle up and stitch the second piece of yarn back on itself. In opposite hands, grasp the ends of both yarns and softly tug until the yarn in the middle joins. When the yarn is paired, you can have to cut the frayed ends.

All of these approaches produce very solid joints in your crocheted cloth that are nearly undetectable. You will find a touch of extra weight when you are using a bulky yarn where the yarn is joined, but not enough to distract from your finished job.

CHAPTER 4:
HOW TO READ A CROCHET PATTERN?

If you are new to crocheting, trying to read a crochet pattern can seem like reading a foreign language. However, don't let this task of understanding crochet patterns stop you from trying your hand at this incredible craft. You have to learn how to read crochet patterns once you learn the basics of crocheting. A whole new world of crochet will open up for you when you learn how to read crochet patterns. You will be able to improve your skillset and move up beyond just the basics. Some patterns of crocheting are designed aimed at beginners, while some are designed for those who are at a more advanced level.

This chapter aims to help you master the new language of crocheting by helping you read crochet patterns irrespective of whether you are new at crocheting or someone who is just looking for a refresher. There are usually a few similarities between all kinds of crochet patterns. Almost all of them begin with a foundation chain from which you work on all the other stitches. Apart from this, some patterns begin with a chainless foundation, where you can make your chain and stitches simultaneously and finish the first row.

Mistakes Crochets Make and Solution

As a beginner, you must come across your fair share of frustrations as you get stuck into your crocheting. Mistakes could happen by not following instructions accurately, or simply as a result of practice. Remember, there are certain methods you can adjust slightly to suit you, as long as they don't affect the appearance of your stitches and your pattern.

Learning to crochet can be a wonderful experience, so try not to get too despondent if you don't always manage to do everything properly at first. It is a very time-consuming craft and requires a lot of skill which you will develop over time. Don't be too hard on yourself and just have fun.

Perhaps you may not be familiar with some of these depending on how much crocheting you have done up to this point. Read through them and keep them in mind if you ever have any of these challenges in the future.

Inserting Your Hook Into the Wrong Chain When You Start

Don't count the first chain on the hook because it is just a loop, your first proper chain is the first chain from the hook which is the one next to and the one after that is the second loop on the hook.

When You Use US Stitches When Your Pattern Contains UK Pattern Terms

This can sometimes be easy to miss and cause several complications. An easy way to check is to look out for single crochet instruction as this confirms that your pattern is a US pattern that uses US terminology.

Not Considering Blocking as an Important Step

First of all, blocking involves handwashing an item and then pinning it into place on a blocking mat. The reason for doing this is to straighten the item and flatten it if needed. It is possible to machine wash your item, just use the hand setting. There are times when blocking isn't completely necessary, whereas so for you. If you intend to wash it then be sure to use the blocked gauge measurements.

Making Starting Loops Using Linked Chains and Not a Magic Loop

You could use methods of starting your crocheting in the round. The first is to work four or five chain stitches and join them in a circle by using a slipstitch. This is the simplest method.

However, a more effective method is to start loops using a magic circle. The center of the circle is much tighter than that of a regular circle linked by a chain stitch. The important thing to remember is consistency, if you use motifs on any items, only use one method to create them as your work will be tidier. So, try both and see which one you feel more comfortable with and stick to that method.

Not Changing the Size of Your Hook as Needed

You may have done this and only realized it when your work didn't look quite right. This can happen when your starting chain is rather tight in comparison to the rest of your work. This is, however, a common mistake among beginners. You must have the right tension in your chain as it forms the foundation of your work.

One solution is to use a slightly larger hook than recommended in your pattern as this will help you to have a more even tension throughout. It is not necessary to change the size of your hook if your tension is correct. Always be aware of specific crochet hook sizes on your patterns.

Your Work Seems to Be Shrinking

If you find that your work is shrinking in places and the shape of your item doesn't look right, then you have probably made an error somewhere. The explanation for a mistake such as this is usually a result of making your first stitch in the incorrect position.

Remember these points:

For a single crochet, the first stitch is inserted into the first stitch of the row above.

For your other basic stitches, it is the turning chain that is to be counted as the first stitch. Hence, this first stitch is inserted into what is the second one of the previous rows.

Not Being Able to Identify Your Stitches

It is common for beginners to be so involved in trying to follow the instructions in their patterns that they seldom check to see whether their stitches actually look the way they should. Never fear, this is quite normal, and a mistake made by so many of us. There are lots of different moving parts and it takes a while to catch your rhythm. When you first start crocheting, take a moment to count your stitches and learn what they look like.

Avoiding New Techniques Because They Seem Too Difficult

If something seems too difficult, look at it more carefully before avoiding it completely. If you can do the basic stitches, you'll be able to handle nearly all the crochet techniques without any problem. You may just need to practice a few times. The steps can sometimes seem a bit intimidating, but if you read through them, you'll see that they are made up of basic instructions. So, don't avoid trying something new, it may be easier than you think, and you'll be able to take your crochet to a new level before you know it!

Not Learning Enough About Yarn

When you start buying yarns, learn as much as you can about them. You will, of course, have to use certain yarns depending on the patterns you are using. But also try and find out which ones are of good quality and don't always go for the cheapest.

You don't realize that your turning chain is the same height as the first stitch in the row.

You should be able to see that the starting chain of your row brings the height of your work up to that of the first stitch in that row. For example, single crochet is one chain and half double crochet is two chains. Have a look at this the next time you are crocheting.

Not Being Able to Read Patterns

Nowadays, you can tend to be a tad bit lazy when it comes to reading patterns. This is because online videos are much quicker and easier to follow for some of us. However, this is not ideal, as you should be able to read patterns. By reading through the pattern steps, you'll be able to create a picture in your mind of what the pattern should look like and it will give you a better understanding of what you are doing.

Not Learning Corner-to-Corner (C2C) Crochet

The C2C method is an important and useful one to learn. You will most definitely use it many times and it is great for making blankets and other garments. Don't avoid this one, try it and practice, and you won't be sorry you did.

Not Learning How to Crochet in the Round

It is important to see how this works and then try it. This is vital to improving your crochet skills, so don't put off learning how to crochet in the round. It is a valuable technique to know how to use.

Not Learning How to Weave in Ends Properly

This is one of the most common mistakes made by beginners. It is so easy to just tie knots to the ends, but this is not the proper way of doing it and it is not neat either. Learn to weave the ends into the surface by using the tapestry needle to finish your work off.

Worrying About Your Mistakes

Making mistakes is what helps you to learn and improve your work. Lots of practice and even more patience, as well as some creativity, is what makes a successful crochet. You will have to undo your stitches from time to time, or even start over again, but that is fine. You are not only learning how to follow instructions; you are also getting used to using your tools and materials so be patient.

Trying Out Complex Patterns First

So often, ladies are in a hurry to create the most beautiful colorful garments without being able to master the stitches or change their yarn colors. This could result in a disaster which could also be incredibly discouraging. Just keep it simple until you are confident with basic crochet work.

Giving Up Too Soon

It is too easy to just pick up your crochet hook, try out a few stitches, and then give up if they don't work. You might feel as though you are getting nowhere, but that is not true. Give yourself plenty of time to learn the basics because once you can do that, then you can move forward and make so many items. If you cannot get your basic stitches right, then you will have problems making your item. Take it easy and things will slowly start coming together.

Even the most skillful people struggled at first, so go for it and enjoy it!

CHAPTER 5:
HAT PATTERNS

Pink Hat

Materials

- 1 skein Old Rose Cotton Yarn (145 meters)—I used .00 mm crochet hook gansilyo

Guro's Milk Cotton Yarn 6

- Tapestry needle
- Scissors

Abbreviations

- SC—single crochet
- DC—double crochet
- TC—treble crochet
- Dec—decrease

Note: Join—always slip stitch on top of the first chain (counted as 1 sc, dc, or tc)

Instructions

Band:

1. Start with the band. Take your 6.00 hook and crochet 75 chains. Join to make a circle.
2. Row 1: CH 1, SC in each stitch around the join. (75 sc)
3. Row 2:6: CH 1, SC in each stitch around (back loops only), join. (75 sc)

Body:

1. Row 1: CH 2, DC in each stitch around, join. (75 dc)
2. Row 2: CH 1, SC in each stitch around, join. (75 sc)
3. Row 3: CH 3, * TC in the second stitch from hook, TC in the first stitch from hook (this will give an X look), repeat * around, join. (37 X clusters or 75 tc)
4. Row 4: CH 1, SC in each stitch around, join. (75 sc)
5. 19–20: repeat rows 1 to 2.
6. Hat closing: decrease sc in back loops only
7. Row 21: CH 1, 3 SC in the next 3 stitches, SC dec in the next 2 stitches, * 4 SC in the next 4 stitches, SC dec in the next 2 stitches, repeat * around, join. (50 sc)
8. Row 22: CH 1, 2 SC in the next 2 stitches, SC dec in the next 2 stitches, * 3 SC in the next 3 stitches, SC dec in the next 2 stitches, repeat * around, join. (40 sc)
9. Row 23: CH 1, SC in the next stitch, SC dec in the next 2 stitches, * 2 SC in the next 2 stitches, SC dec in the next 2 stitches, repeat * around, join. (30 sc)

10. Row 24: CH 1, SC dec in the next 2 stitches, * SC in the next stitch, SC dec in the next 2 stitches, repeat * around, (20 sc)

11. Row 25: CH 1, SC dec in the next 2 stitches around, (10 sc)

12. Row 26: CH 1, SC in all stitches around (10 sc)

13. Fasten off and weave ends with a tapestry needle.

Basic Baby Beanie

Materials

Directions are for two sizes of the hat—a small hat for children 2–4 years old and a larger hat for children 4–12 years old

- Worsted-weight yarn
- Crochet hook, size H/8; 6
- Tapestry needle

Instructions

1. Round 1: Chain 3. Crochet 13 double crochets in the first chain. Join with a slip stitch to the top of the chain. You will have 14 stitches.
2. Round 2: Chain 2. Crochet 1 forward post double crochet. Crochet 1 double crochet stitch in each stitch in the round. Join with a slip stitch to the top of the chain. You will have 28 stitches.
3. Round 3: Chain 2. Crochet in each forward post double chain. Crochet 1 double crochet stitch in each stitch in the round. Join with a slip stitch to the top of the chain. You will have 28 stitches.
4. Round 4: Chain 2. Crochet in each forward post double chain. Crochet 2 double

crochet stitches in each stitch in the round. Join with a slip stitch to the top of the chain. You will have 42 stitches.

5. Round 5: Chain 2. Crochet in each forward post double crochet. Crochet double crochet stitches on top of the forward post double chain. Join with a slip stitch to the top of the chain. You will have 56 stitches.

6. Round 6: Chain 2. Crochet in each forward post double crochet. Crochet double crochet in each double crochet. Repeat the round. Join with a slip stitch to the top of the chain. You will have 56 stitches.

7. For the small-size hat, repeat Round 6 for Rounds 7–14. For a larger hat, repeat Round 6 for Rounds 16–18.

Finish:

1. Crochet one forward post double chain in the forward post double chain. Then forward post in a double chain and back post in a double chain. Repeat this pattern for the round. Join with a slip stitch at the end of the row. Finish off.

Hat Spikes

Materials

- Weighted-worsted yarn
- Crochet hook, size G/6; 4.0
- Yarn needle

Instructions

Note: This pattern is for one spike. Repeat to make the number of spikes that you want to add to your hat.

2. Round 1: Crochet 3. Slip stitch to join round. Chain 1. Single crochet 6 stitches into the round. You now have 6 stitches.
3. Round 2: Crochet 1 single crochet in the first stitch, single crochet two into the next stitch. Continue this pattern for the rest of the round. You will have 9 stitches.
4. Round 3: Crochet 1 single crochet into each stitch for the rest of the round. You will have 9 stitches.

5. Round 4: Crochet 1 single crochet into the next two stitches, single crochet two stitches into the next stitch. Continue this pattern for the rest of the round. You will have 12 stitches.

6. Round 5: Crochet 1 single crochet into each stitch for the rest of the round. You will have 12 stitches.

7. Round 6: Crochet 1 single crochet into the first three stitches, single crochet two stitches into the next stitch. Continue this pattern for the rest of the round. You will have 15 stitches.

8. Round 7: Crochet 1 single crochet into each stitch for the rest of the round. You will have 15 stitches.

9. Round 8: Crochet 1 single crochet into the first four stitches, single crochet two into the next stitch, and continue this pattern for the rest of the round. You will have 18 stitches.

10. Round 9: Crochet 1 single crochet into each stitch for the rest of the round. You will have 18 stitches. Slip stitch into the next single crochet. Fasten off. Leave a 6-inch length of yarn to attach the spike to the hat.

Attaching spikes:

1. Arrange completed spikes down the outside center of the hat. Use the 6-inch length of yarn to securely attach each spike on the inside.

Hat Flower

Materials

- Light-weight yarn, any color
- Crochet hook, size G/6; 4.0
- Yarn needle

Instructions

These directions will make one rose. Repeat to make the number of roses that you want for your hat.

Tip: This hat uses a V stitch. A V stitch is worked in one space. It consists of one double crochet stitch, 1 chain, and 1 more double crochet.

1. Row 1: Crochet a chain of 45. In the third chain, complete a V stitch, and then chain 1, skip 1, and V stitch in the next chain. This pattern will be used for the rest of the row. Chain 1 and turn. You will have 21 V stitches.
2. Crochet 7 double crochets into V stitch. Slip stitch into the chain, skip one, chain

one, 7 double chains into V stitch, repeat until the last 2 V stitches. Slip stitch into chain 1 space, chain 1, 6 half-double crochet stitches into V space, slip stitch into chain 1 space, crochet 5 half double crochet stitches into last v space, slip stitch into beginning chain.

Fasten off:

1. Leave a long length of yarn for sewing. You will have 21 petals.
2. Carefully roll the petals so that they radiate from the center out. Sew the bottom of the petals together to hold the shape.

Party Spirals for Hat

Materials

- Any yarn
- Any hook
- Crochet needle

Instructions

This pattern will make one spiral. Change colors and make as many spirals as you want for your hat.

1. Crochet a chain of 25. In the third chain from the crochet hook, double crochet 7 stitches.
2. In the next chain, double crochet 8 stitches.
3. In the next chain, double crochet 8 stitches. Continue to the end of the chain.

Finish off:

1. Leave a 6-inch tail to attach the spiral to the hat.

2. Position spirals to the very top of the hat. Sew a 6-inch tail to the inside of the hat. Weave ends.

Bear Ears for Hat

Materials

- Medium worsted-weight yarn
- Crochet hook H/8; 5.0
- Crochet needle

Instructions

Make two ears.

1. Chain 4. Slip stitch ends to form a ring.
2. Round 1: Chain 1. Crochet 8 single crochet stitches into the ring. Slip stitch to join. You will have 8 stitches.
3. Round 2: Chain 1. Crochet 2 single crochets into each single crochet stitch. Slip stitch to join. You will have 16 stitches.

4. Round 3: Chain 1. Crochet 1 single crochet into each stitch. You will have 16 stitches. Finish off. Leave a long tail of yarn.

5. Sew both ears to each side of the beanie. Weave ends.

Versatile Headband

Materials

- Any yarn
- Any hook

Instructions

1. Measure the size of the head that you are making the headband for baby to adult. Follow this pattern until you reach the desired length.
2. Chain 11.
3. Row 1: Slip stitch into the 5th chain. Chain 2. Skip 2. Slip stitch into the next chain. Chain 3. Skip 2. Slip stitch into the next chain. Chain 4. Turn. You will have 4 ovals in this row.
4. Row 2: Slip stitch into 3rd chain. Chain 3. Slip stitch into chain 2nd space. Chain 3. Slip stitch into the last chain space. Chain 4. Turn. You will have 3 ovals in this row.
5. Row 3: Slip stitch into the 4th chain stitch. Chain 3. Slip stitch into 3rd chain space. Chain 4. Slip stitch into 4th chain space. Chain 4. Turn. You will have 3 ovals in this row.
6. Repeat Row 3 until you crocheted your headband to the desired length.
7. Place the right sides together. Join with a slip stitch.
8. Turn the right side out and your headband is ready!

Ring of Shells Headband

Materials

- 4-ply worsted-weight soft yarn
- Crochet hook, size H/8; 6

Instructions

These directions are for a six-month-old child. To make a larger or smaller headband, measure the head that you are making the headband for and crochet chains in step 1 to the desired length. The number of chains must be divisible by 4.

1. Crochet 44 loose chains.
2. Pattern- In the third chain, crochet 3 double crochet stitches in the same chain. Skip a chain, slip stitch in the next chain, skip a chain, crochet 4 double crochet stitches in the next chain, skip a chain, and crochet 4 double-crochets stitches in the next chain. Repeat this pattern until the end of the chain. Turn.
3. Repeat the pattern in step two, but this time, crocheting into the lower loop of the original chain. The emerging pattern should be a symmetrical ring of shells on the top and bottom of the chains. Fasten off leaving a 6-inch tail.
4. Place the right sides together and weave the tail into a slip stitch that joins the headband. Weave in end.
5. Turn right side out.

Baby Pom Pom Hat

Materials

- 1 x 100g ball of Soft Merino Aran (100% merino superwash)
- 4.5 mm crochet hook
- Tapestry needle
- 4 or 6 small pom poms (2 or 3 for each side of the hat) 5cm/2 in. Diameter.

Instructions

1. Row 1: Treble crochet (tr) until the end of the row.
2. Next row: Don't forget that treble crochet requires a turning chain of 3 chains at the beginning of each new row.
3. Continue to work treble crochet (tr) along each row until your panel measures the

correct size and is a square (height of work same as width). Fasten off.

4. Repeat to make a second identical panel.

Sewing up your hat:

1. Lay the first crocheted panel with the right side—what will ultimately be the outside of the hat—facing up. Now lay the second-panel face down on top so that the 'right side' of each panel is touching.
2. Make sure the foundation chain/bottom edge of each panel matches up. Starting on the left side sew both panels together—left side, across the top and right side, leaving the bottom seams open.
3. Turn the hat right sides out.
4. Thread a tapestry needle with spare yarn and use it to gather the right corner of the hat before sewing the pom poms very securely to the hat. Repeat for the left corner of the hat.

Crown Hat

Work each round with a different color to create the rainbow effect of the hat. Join all rounds with a slip stitch in the first stitch.

With the first color in chain four, join a slip stitch to form a ring or begin with Magic Ring.

Materials

- Products Yarn: worsted wool yarn 60 yards / 28 gr. The comparison uses Swish Worsted Knit Picks in Conch.
- Crochet hook: Scale I/9—crochet hook 5, 50 mm (adjust to get the correct gauge).
- Other: needle tapestry to weave in ends.

1. Step 1: Chain three (counts as double crochet), two double crochet in the ring, [chain one, three double crochet into the ring] repeat three times, chain one, join it with slip stitch to the top of chain three-four shells, four chains once spaces. Fasten off.
2. Step 2: With the following color (standing double crochet, five double crochet) in any chain one space (counts as the start of shell, shell), two shells.
3. Following three chains, one space, join the eight shells and then fasten off.
4. Continuing this, 'space' refers to the space between three double crochet shells. It is

not a chain space.

5. Step 3: With the next color, the start of the shell in the first space (between double shells), two shells in the next space,

6. [Shell in the next space, two shells in the next space] three times, join—12 shells, and then fasten off.

7. Step 4: With the next color, starting shell in any space, shell in each space around, join. Fasten off.

8. Step 5: With the next color, start a shell in any space between shells, shell in the next space, two shells in, next space, [shell in following two spaces, two shells in the next space] around, join—16 shells. Fasten off.

9. Step 6: With the next color, starting shell in any space, shell in each space around, join. Fasten off.

10. Step 7: With the next color (starting shell, shell) in any space, [shell in following two spaces, two shells in the next space] 3 times, shell in each space to end, join—21 shells. Fasten off.

11. Step 8: With the next color, starting shell in any space, shell in each space around, join.

Fasten off:

1. Repeat the last round until the hat measures 7¾' [19.5 cm] from the top.

2. Last Step: With the next color or colors you want to use for edging, start a shell in any space, shell in each space around, and join.

Edging:

1. Step 1–2: Chain one crochet in each stitch around and join. Weave in ends.

Free Crochet Headband

Materials

- Products Yarn: worsted wool yarn 60 yards / 28 gr. The comparison uses Swish Worsted Knit Picks in Conch.
- Crochet hook: Scale I/9—crochet hook 5, 50 mm (adjust to get the correct gauge).
- Other: needle tapestry to weave in ends.

The completed headband measures about 19 'in diameter. At its narrowest point in front, it measures about 2–¼ inches high and 3–½ inches long at the highest point in the back. You may change the diameter at the end of each segment by adding or removing a row.

Measure the job after the first 5 rows of the pattern. You need a square of around 2–¼ inches long. Consider using a small crochet hook if it is larger. Use a large crochet hook if it is smaller.

Stitch variation:

This headband pattern uses a half-double stitch variation in which you are operating only in the back loops of the stitches.

Style notes:

Ch 2 for the turning chain between each board; the turning chain is 1 hdc st in all.

This headband begins in the middle of the piece and works backward; you then rotate the work and crochet the mirror image of the first half of the piece.

By breaking the yarn and beginning in the middle, you can stop weaving in extra ends. Pull approximately 30 meters of yarn and wind it in a ball, then start to crochet. You can use them later with some free scrap yarn patterns if you finish up with yarn leftovers.

Instructions

1. Divide the yarn and make the starting slip knots—a job with the little ball yarn ch 10.

2. Row 1: hdc in the third ch of the hook and every ch over. The first two chs in the row are the first hdc st, which gives you 9 hdc sts in total.

3. Rows 2–6: Work hdc over blo for each st. In each row, you will have a total of 9 m.

4. Row 7: Work the hdc over the block in each st. Take 2 hdc sts to the turning chain at the end of this line for a total of 10 m in a row.

5. Row 8: In through st, function hdc via blo = 10 m in a row.

6. Row 9: Work 2 hdc sts into turning chain for 11 sts at the end of row.

7. Line 10: Job hdc in through st by blo. Total = 11 m in line.

8. Row 11: Work 2 sts hdc in turning chain at row end for a total of 12 sts in row.

9. Row 12: In through st, work hdc via blo = 12 sts in row.

10. Row 13: Work half a double crochet column—work 2 hdc sts for a total of 13 m in the row into the turning chain.

11. Row 14: Function hdc in through st through the blood = 13 meters in a row.

12. Row 15: Work 2 hdc sts on turning chain at the row end for 14 m in a row.

13. Rows 16–20: Work hdc in each st by block = 14 m in each row.

14. You can add an extra row if you want to create a bigger headband.

15. Function fewer rows here to make a smaller headband.

16. Bring in the active loop to a safety pin or stitch marker.

17. Switch the job and go back to the side with the starting chain to make the other half of the headband.

18. Row 21: Take a loop and ch 2 with the yarn connected to the skein. Work back through the start chain and work 1 hdc in the free band of each st in the string.

19. Total = 9 sts hdc.

20. Rows 22–26: Rep lines 2–6.

21. Row 27: Increase by one stitch at the beginning of the section. To do this, work 2 hdcs into the bl of the first st. In this line and the rest of the pattern, make your increases like this. Finish the rest of the row by working hdc in each st in the row after through. Total = 10 M. Total.

22. Row 28: Job hdc in any st by block = 10 m in a row.

23. Row 29: Increase by one stitch at the beginning of the line. Total = 11 m in rows.

24. Row 30: Function hdc over every st by block = 11 m in a row. Row 30:

25. Row 31: Increase by one stitch at the beginning of the section. Total = row 12 sts.

26. Row 32: In through st, function hdc via blo = 12 meters in section.

27. Row 33: Increase by one stitch at the beginning of the line. Overall = 13 m in a row.

28. Row 34: In each line, job hdc by blo = 13 sts in row.

29. Row 35: Increase by one stitch at the beginning of the range. Total = 14 m in rows.

30. Rows 36–40: Function hdc in each st by block = 14 m in each row.

31. If, in the first half of the project, you added additional rows after row 20, please add the same number of rows at the end too.

32. In your active loop, place a safety pin or stitch marker.

33. If the headband is not a gift, you can easily check and make sure that the checks are all right. Secure the sides of the headband with safety pins and put it on the intended recipient. Make some changes until the headband is done.

34. Finish the headband and keep together the two ends of the headband and secure it with a slip stitch. You may also use a whip stitch or other form of connection. Weave in ends.

Optional: You can apply slip stitches to both borders if you want to make the upper and lower edges of the belt look cleaner and done. The slip stitches do not stretch far, however, so the fit is affected. If you want to add your slip stitches, add them and work with loose, simple tension before tying the yarn.

Brown and Fuzzy Earflap Bonnet

Materials

- 1 ball of light and lofty yarn or super bulky weight yarn (brown stripes)
- 10 mm crochet hook

Gauge

- Finished hat size fit for a baby with 16'-19' inch head circumference.

Instructions

Make the hat:

2. In Round 1: chain 2, 6 single crochet in the second chain from hook, join beginning single crochet with a slip stitch.
3. In Round 2: chain 2, 2 double crochet in every single crochet, join with slip stitch. (Total:12 double crochet)
4. Round 3: chain 2, * 1 double crochet in the next double crochet, 2 double crochet in the next double crochet*, repeat * around, join with slip stitch. (Total:18 double crochet)
5. Round 4: chain 2, *1 double crochet in the next 2 double crochet, 2 double crochet in the next double crochet*, repeat * around, join with slip stitch. (Total:24 double crochet)
6. Round 5: chain 2, *1 double crochet in the next 3 double crochet, 2 double crochet in the next double crochet*, repeat * around, join with slip stitch. (Total:30 double crochet)
7. Rounds 6–8: chain 2, 1 double crochet in each double crochet around, join with slip stitch. (Total:30 double crochet)

Make the earflaps:

1. Row 1: chain 2, 1 double crochet in the next 6 double crochet (Total:6 double crochet), turn.
2. Row 2: chain 2, 2 double crochets together, 1 double crochet, 2 double crochet

together. (Total:3 double crochet), finish off

3. Skip 10 double crochet and reconnect yarn to work on the second earflap.

4. Finishing: single crochet around the edge and finish off

Newborn Crochet Hat

Materials

- Yarn weight: 3 (Light/DK).
- Crochet hook: 6 mm/J.

Instructions

1. Round 1: Create a circle then make ch 3 and 11 dc in the said circle until 12 stitches.

2. Round 2: Make 1 dc and ch 3 in the first stitch then 2 dc in every stitch all the way around until you reach 24 stitches.

3. Round 3: Next, make ch 3 and 2 dc in the next stitch. Make 1 dc in the next stitch and 2 dc in the other, then repeat from to all the way around until it reaches 3 ½ inches.

4. Round 4–10: Ch 3 in 1 dc for every stitch in the round.

5. Round 11: Make ch 1 and 1 sc for each stitch. Then, make 1 sc for each of the next 8 stitches and 2 sc in the next Repeat from to all the way and make sl stitch to join.

6. Round 12 onwards: Make 1 sc and ch 1 for every stitch in the round and then continue until you reach the diameter that would suit the baby's head.

Bulky Ski Bonnet

Materials

- 1 skein of super bulky weight yarn (blue)
- P or 11.5mm crochet hook
- Tapestry needle

Gauge

- With P hook, 4 half double crochet = 2'

Instructions

1. Make the hat base.
2. Make 21 chains, single crochet in the 2nd hook, and single crochet in each chain to end. Turn. Total: 20 single crochet.
3. In Row 1: Chain 1, half double crochet in each stitch across, turn 20 (20, 24, 24) half double crochet.
4. Repeat Row 1 until the hat measures 14' from the beginning, or until the hat fits the wearer.
5. In the last row: Fold your crocheted hat until the long edges are aligned. Chain 1, slip stitch through the next stitch working through both edges of the fabric to hold the piece together.
6. Continue from the pattern in Row 1 across the next 19 stitches. Fasten off
7. Make the edging of the hat.
8. Attach yarn to an open end. Work 28 single crochet stitches evenly spaced around the opening. Use the method of 2 stitches per inch to evenly space your single crochet.
9. Fasten off. Be sure to weave in every loose end.
10. Attach the pompom.
11. Cut a 24' long length of yarn. This piece of yarn should be laced through the stitches 1.5' below the opening without edging.
12. Tightly pull the yarn to make a gathered 'pompom' effect.
13. Tie off in a tight bow as desired.
14. Fold up the bottom 4 or 5 rows to form the cuff.

Fuzzy Bear Baby Beanie

Materials

- Crochet hook 5.5 mm or you can use 1/9
- Yarn weight chunky/bulky (five) mostly 12–17 stitches for 4 inches
- For materials make use of a yarn needle, and a hook, while for the bulky yarn I make use of Bernat baby breath.

Instructions

1. Ch 4 sl st into the 1st ch. (the hat is usually worked in a round cycle.) It would be a safe idea to have a long sufficient tail to double as a pattern maker.
2. Round 1: hdc in 9x ch4 rounds. Ensure that you place a marker to enable get to where the round will end.
3. Round 2: ensure that 2hdc are in each of the st mostly around the marker.
4. Round 3: hdc in each st around, place marker (17 hdc).
5. Round 4: replicate row 2 (36–37 hdc) rnd.
6. Round 5–11: hdc in st around (36 hdc).
7. Round 12: hdc st around to marker, sc in the next st, sl, st in the next tie off as well as weave in ends.
8. Ear part (make 2)
9. Ch 4, sl st in 1st ch row 1—7 hdc in ch 4 sp, ch 1, turn row 2—0–3 month—sc in each st around, tie off.

Ear side:

1. Place the hat down on the table as well as place the ears such that the edge of the ear is between the bottom of round 2 as well as the bottom of round 5.
2. Stitch the remaining end of the ear down as well as weave the edge or ends in the inside of the hat by linking the two strands (one from the start of the ch for the ears and another from the finishing tail) together, stitching the remaining end of the ear down before weaving the ends in the inner part of the hat.

Simple Pink Beret

Materials

- 1 skein of worsted-weight yarn in pink
- G-sized crochet hook

Gauge

- 9 double crochet = 2inches
- 7 rnds = 3 inches

Instructions

1. Make the beret's crown.
2. Chain 4. To join, work a slip stitch to form a ring.
3. In round 1: chain 3, 13 double crochet in ring, join with a slip stitch to the top of chain-3. 14 double crochet counting chain-3 and double crochet.
4. In round 2: chain 3, double crochet in the same stitch with chain-3, 2dc in each stitch around. Join each round with a slip stitch (slip stitch) to the top of chain-3, 28 double crochet.
5. In round 3: chain 3, 2dc in the next stitch, double crochet in the next stitch, 2dc in the next stitch; rep from around. 42dc.
6. In Round 4: chain 3, double crochet in the next stitch, 2dc in the next stitch, double crochet in the next 2 stitches, 2dc in the next stitch, and repeat from around. 56dc.
7. In Round 5: chain 3, double crochet in each of the next 2 stitches, 2dc in the next stitch, double crochet in each of the next 3 stitches, 2 double crochet in the next stitch; repeat from around.70dc.
8. Continue the process to increase 14 stitches every round, having 1 stitch more between increases each round until there are 8 (9,10) stitches between increases.
9. Work 3 rounds even.
10. Decrease the beret.
11. Make the 1st decrease. Round: Work 8 (9, 10) stitches, draw up a loop in each of the next 2 stitches, yo (yarn over), and through 3 loops on hook (1 stitch decrease); rep from around. Join.

12. Make the 2nd decrease Round: Work 7 (8, 9) stitches, decrease; rep from around. Join.

13. Continue the process to decrease 14 stitches every round, having 1 stitch less between decreases each round until there are 6 stitches between decreases.

14. Crochet the headband.

15. Work 6 rounds of one single crochet in each stitch.

16. Join and fasten off.

Christmas Knit Hat Pattern

Materials

- Size 6 US (4.25 mm) 16' circular needles
- Size 6 US (4.25 mm) double points
- One ball Splash (Color White #101) by Crystal Palace Yarns
- 100% polyester
- 94 yards/100 grams
- 2 skeins cotton Chenille (Color Apple Red #8166) by Crystal Palace Yarns
- 100% mercerized cotton
- 98 yards/50 grams

Gauge

- 16 sts = 4' in St with Cotton Chenille

Instructions

1. With Splash and circular needles, CO 70 (60) sts. Join being careful not to twist. Place marker for beg of round.
2. Knit with Splash for 9 rounds.
3. Change to Cotton Chenille and knit in St st for 7' for the crown of the hat.
4. Begin dec rows as follows (when the diameter gets too small for circular needles, change to the double point needles).
5. K8, k2tog; rep from
6. Knit 8 (7) rounds
7. K7, k2tog; rep from
8. Knit 8(7) rounds
9. K6, k2tog; rep from
10. Knit 8 (7) rounds
11. K5, k2tog; rep from
12. Knit 8 (7) rounds
13. K4, k2tog; rep from
14. Knit 4 (3) rounds

15. K3, k2tog; rep from
16. Knit 4 (3) rounds
17. K2, k2tog; rep from
18. Knit 4 (3) rounds
19. K1, k2tog; rep from
20. Knit 2 (2) rounds
21. K2tog around until 1 st remains and fasten off.
22. Make a Splash Pom-Pom and attach it.

Crochet a Pink Bow

1. With Pink yarn, make 20 chains.
2. Row 1: single crochet in the 3rd stitch from the hook, single crochet in each stitch along the row.
3. Row 2: Turn, Chain 1, single crochet in each stitch along the row.
4. Make 4 more rows using the pattern in Row 2.
5. Leave 8' or 20.5 cm yarn before cutting to be used to sew the ribbon together with the hat.
6. The ring in the middle should be tied with a piece of pink yarn to make a bow.
7. Sew it parallel to the pink stripe imitating the ribbon.

Hooded Baby Blanket

Materials

This blanket is 28 inches square

- 16 ounces 4-ply soft yarn
- Crochet hook J-10; 6.0
- Tapestry needle

Instructions

Blanket:

1. Chain 108 stitches. You will work Row 1 and Row 2 in a textured pattern until crocheted fabric measures 28 inches in length. Finish off. Weave ends.
2. Row 1: Crochet 2 double crochets into the 3rd chain, skip 2 chains, crochet 1 single crochet stitch and 2 double crochets in the next chain, skip the next two chains, and repeat across the row. Single crochet in the last chain. Chain 2 and turn.
3. Row 2: Double crochet in the first stitch, skip the next two stitches, crochet 1 single crochet and 2 double crochets in the next stitch, skip the next 2 stitches, and repeat across the row. Single crochet on top of turning stitch.

Hood:

1. Chain 4. Row 1: Crochet 2 double crochet stitches into the 4th chain. Chain 3 and turn.
2. Row 2: Crochet 2 double crochets in the first stitch, 1 double crochet in the next stitch, and crochet 3 double crochets on top of the turning chain. You should have 7 double crochet stitches. Chain 3 and turn.
3. Row 3: Crochet 1 double crochet in the first stitch and 1 double crochet in each stitch of the row. Crochet 2 double crochets on top of the turning chain. You should have 9 double crochets. Chain 3 and turn.
4. Row 4: Crochet 2 double crochets in the first stitch. Crochet 1 double crochet in each stitch of the row. Crochet 3 double crochets on top of the turning chain. You should have 13 double crochets.

5. Repeat Rows 3 and 4 six times. You will have 49 double crochets. Place the hood over one corner of the blanket, right sides together. Sew together with yarn and tapestry needle.

Blanket trim:

1. In contrasting colors, or the same color, single crochet every stitch at the edge of the blanket and hood. Stitch two single crochets in each corner. Finish off. Slip stitch to join. Weave in end.

Hoodie Hat

Materials

- Needles: US 17
- Yarn: 4, medium weight, about 50 total grams, 4 strands
- Extra: Yarn needle, fun yarn (about 10 yards)

Gauge

- 16 S in 4 inches, not required but advisable

Instructions

1. With the 4 strands, cast on 22 stitches.
2. Knit each row until you make a 24-inch wide rectangle.
3. Cast off with 15 inches of a yarn tail.
4. Fold your rectangle in half and sew the back seam together with the yarn needle. Turn the hat right-side out so that the seam is on the inside.
5. Add fun yarn to the two sides of the hat so that it hangs down by the ears in tassels and one long tassel at the top, if you want.
6. To make a tassel:
7. With fun yarn, wrap it around your 4 fingers approximately 20 times. Tie securely through the loop.
8. Tie a second piece of yarn towards the top of the bundle where it is tied together so there is a small ball formed at the top.
9. Trim the ends of the tassel so they are loose.
10. Insert the ends of the tie holding the bundle together at the sides and on the top of your hat and tie securely on the inside. Intertwine the ends into the finished
11. Work.

Frog Eye Hat Knit Pattern

Materials

- Size 5 dpns or size to get gauge
- Worsted-weight green yarn.
- Darning needle.

Gauge

- Stitch gauge: 1 inch = 4.75 sts x 7 rows on size 5 needles
- 2×2 ribbing—k2, p2
- PCB3—Purl Cable Back 3: slip one to the cable needle, and hold it back. K2, then p1 from cable needle
- PCF3—Purl Cable Front 3: slip two to the cable needles, and hold to the front. P1, then k2 from cable needle
- PCB4—Purl Cable Back 4: Slip 2 sts to cable needle, hold to back, p2, k2 from cable needle
- PCF4—Purl Cable Front 4: Slip 2 sts to cable needle, hold to front, p2, k2 from cable needle

Instructions

1. Using longtail or another stretchy cast-on method, cast on 80 [88 96] sts. Spread stitches equally across 4 needles.
2. Work 12 rows in a 2×2 rib.

Cable pattern:

1. On even rows, k in k sts, p in p sts. You do four repeats of the parenthesis.
2. Rows 1 -4: (p4 [5 6], k2, p8 [9 10], k2, p4)
3. Row 5: (p4 [5 6], k2, p7 [8 9], k4, p3)
4. Row 7: (p4 [5 6], k2, p6 [7 8], PCB3, PCF3, p2)
5. Row 9: (p4 [5 6], k2, p4 [5 6], PCB4, p2, PCF4)
6. Row 11: (p4 [5 6], k2, p4 [5 6], k2, p6, k2)
7. Row 13: (p4 [5 6], k2, p4 [5 6], PCF4, p2, PCB4)

8. Row 15: (p4 [5 6], k2, p6 [7 8], PCF3, PCB3, p2)

9. Row 17: (p4 [5 6], k2, p7 [8 9], k4, p3)

10. Row 19: (p4 [5 6], k2, p8 [9 10], k2, p4)

11. Row 21: (p3 [4 5], k4, p7 [8 9], k2, p4)

12. Row 23: (p2 [3 4], PCB3, PCF3, p6 [7 8], k2, p4)

13. Row 25: (p0 [1 2], PCB4, p2, PCF4, p4 [5 6], k2, p4)

14. Row 27: (p0 [1 2], k2, p6, k2, p4 [5 6], k2, p4)

15. Row 29: (p0 [1 2], PCF4, p2, PCB4, p4 [5 6], k2, p4)

16. Row 31: (p2 [3 4], PCF3, PCB3, p6 [7 8], k2, p4)

17. Row 33: (p3 [4 5], k4, p7 [8 9], k2, p4)

18. Row 35: (p4 [5 6], k2, p8 [9 10], k2, p4)

The crown:

1. To do the crown, you'll want to shift your needle placements over. To do so p4,k1. This is the new start of the round. Four repeats of the parenthesis.

2. Row 1: (k1, p7 [8 9], k4, p7 [8 9], k1)

3. Row 3: (ssk, p5 [6 7], PCB3, PCF3, p5 [6 7], k2tog)

4. Row 5: (ssk, p3 [4 5], PCB4, p2, PCF4, p3 [4 5], k2tog)

5. Row 7: (ssk, p1 [2 3], k2, p6, k2, p1 [2 3], k2tog)

6. Row 9: (ssk, p0 [1 2], PCF4, p2, PCB4, p0 [1 2], k2tog)

7. Row 11: (ssk, p1 [2 3], PCF3, PCB3, p1 [2 3], k2tog)

8. Row 13: (ssk, p1 [2 3], k4, p1 [2 3], k2tog)

9. Row 15: (ssk, p1 [2 3], k2, p1 [2 3], k2tog)

10. Row 17: (ssk, k0 [1 2], k2, k0 [1 2], k2tog)

11. Row 19: (ssk, k0 [1 ssk], k2tog)

12. Pull yarn through the remaining stitches. Weave in ends. Finish the hat with a pom-pom.

Pompom Winter Hat

Materials

- Simply Soft (170 g/6. Oz;288 m/315 yds); Contrast A Neon Yellow (9773)—1 ball
- Simply Soft Heathers (141 g/5. Oz;228 m/250 yds); Main Color (MC) Charcoal Heather (9508)—1 ball
- Sizes U.S. 7 (4.5 mm) and U.S. 8 (5 mm) circular knitting needles 16' [40 cm] long
- Set of 4 double-pointed knitting needles, sizes U.S. 8 (5 mm) or size needed to obtain gauge
- Stitch marker

Gauge

- 18 sts and 24 rows = 4' [10 cm] in stocking stitch with larger needles and 1 strand.

Instructions

1. With 2 strands of MC tog and a smaller circular needle, cast on 88 sts. Join in the round, placing the marker on first st.
2. Round 1: Knit.
3. Round 2: Purl.
4. Repeat the last 2 rounds until work from the beginning measures 2½' [6 cm], ending on a knit round.

Latvian braid:

1. Round 1: With 2 strands of MC, K1. With 2 strands of A, K1. Repeat from around.
2. Round 2: With both MC and A held in front of work, With MC, P1. With A, P1. When switching yarns, wrap yarn for the next st under yarn used for the previous st. Repeat around.
3. Round 3: With MC, P1. With A, P1. When switching yarns, wrap yarn for the next st over yarn used for the previous st. Repeat around.
4. Break A and 1 strand of MC.
5. With the remaining 1 strand of MC and a larger circular knitting needle, knit in rounds until work from the beginning measures 6' [15 cm].

6. Shape top, changing to set of 4 double pointed needles where appropriate:

7. Round 1: K9. K2tog. Repeat around. 80 sts.

8. Round 2 and alternate rounds: Knit.

9. Round 3: K8. K2tog. Repeat around. 72 sts.

10. Round 5: K7. K2tog. Repeat form around. 64 sts.

11. Round 7: K6. K2tog. Repeat from around. 56 sts.

12. Round 9: K5. K2tog. Repeat around. 48 sts.

13. Round 1: K4. K2tog. Repeat around. 40 sts.

14. Round 3: K3. K2tog. Repeat around. 32 sts.

15. Round 5: K2. K2tog. Repeat around. 24 sts.

16. Round 7: K1. K2tog. Repeat around. 16 sts.

17. Round 8: k2tog. Repeat around. 8 sts.

18. Break yarn, leaving a long end. Thread end through remaining sts and draw up tightly. Fasten securely.

Pompom:

1. Wrap A around 4 fingers approximately 90 times. Remaining over from fingers and tie tightly in the center. Cut through each side of the loops. Trim to a smooth round shape. Sew to the top of the hat.

Extra Warm Hat Knit Pattern

Materials

- Yarn: Worsted, dk, or any yarn held together in two strands
- 10 ½ circular needles, and #10 or #10 ½ dpn needles to finish the top of the hat

Gauge

- 3 sts/inch. # 10 ½ circular needles

Instructions

1. CO on 60 stitches, join and begin knitting in the round. Work 8 inches, alternating a row of knit, and a row of purl, for garter stitch.
2. Row 1: (Knit 8, K 2 tog) repeat 6 times: 54 sts
3. Row 2 and all even rows: Work even
4. Row 3: (Knit 7, k 2 tog) 6 times: 48 sts
5. Row 5: (Knit 6, k 2 tog) 6 times: 42 sts
6. Row 7: (Knit 5, K 2 tog) 6 times: 36 sts
7. Row 9: (Knit 4, K 2 tog) 6 times: 30 sts
8. Row 11: (Knit 3, K 2 tog) 6 times: 24 sts
9. Row 13: (Knit 2, K2 tog) 6 times: 18 sts
10. Row 15: (Knit 1, K2 tog) 6 times: 12 sts
11. Row 17: (K 2 tog) 6 times: 6 sts
12. Row 18: Knit even
13. Cut yarn, thread tail through remaining 6 sts, and pull. Bring the tail to the inside of the hat, and weave it in.
14. Wear with the brim folded up.

Rainbow Hat

Materials

- 1 oz yellow (A) worsted-weight yarn
- 1 oz green (B) worsted-weight yarn
- 1 oz blue (C) worsted-weight yarn
- 1 oz purple (D) worsted-weight yarn
- 1 oz red or purple-red (E) worsted-weight yarn
- 1 oz orange or melon (F) worsted-weight yarn
- J-sized crochet hook scissors
- Tapestry needle for weaving ends

Gauge

- 5 double crochet = 2' (2 strands)

Instructions

Note: The rainbow hat is crocheted with a double strand of yarn throughout. The colors are based according to the order of the spectrum. Each color is used solid first, then mixed with the next color. Start with any color you prefer.

1. Make the hat starting from the top using 2 strands of yellow yarn.
2. Chain 4, slip stitch in the first chain to form a ring.
3. Round 1: Chain 3 (counts as 1 double crochet), 11 double crochet in the ring. Join each round with a slip stitch on top of chain 3. Cut 1 strand of yellow. Join 1 strand of green.
4. Round 2: With AB, chain 3, double crochet in the same chain with a slip stitch, 2 double crochet in each double crochet around. (Total: 24 double crochet). Cut A. Join another strand of green.
5. Round 3: With 2 green yarns, chain 3, 2 double crochet in the next double crochet, * double crochet in the next double crochet, 2 double crochet in the next double crochet, repeat from * around (Total: 36 double crochet). Cut 1 strand of green. Join 1 strand of blue.

6. Round 4: With green and blue strands, chain 3, double crochet in each double crochet around. Cut green. Join another strand of blue.

7. Round 5: With 2 blue strands, chain 3, double crochet in the same chain with slip stitch. * Double crochet in each of the next 2 double crochet, 2 double crochet in the next double crochet, repeat from * around, end double crochet in each of the last 2 double crochet. (Total: 48 double crochet). Cut 1 strand of blue. Join 1 strand of purple.

8. Round 6: With blue and purple strands, work even. (Total:48 double crochet) Cut C. Join another strand of purple.

9. Round 7: With 2 purple strands, work even. Cut 1 strand of purple. Join 1 strand of red.

10. Round 8: With purple and red strands, work even. Cut purple. Join another strand of red.

11. Round 9: With 2 red strands, work even.

12. Round 10: With 2 red strands, single crochet in each double crochet around. Work loose or tight depending on the wearer's head.

13. Make the hat's brim.

14. Round 11: With 2 red strands, * chain 4, skip 3 single crochet, single crochet in the next single crochet, chain 3, skip 3 single crochet, single crochet in the next single crochet, repeat from * around. (Total: 12 loops). Slip stitch in the first chain. Cut 1 strand of red. Join 1 strand of orange.

15. Round 12: With red and orange strands, chain 3, * 6 double crochet in the next loop, double crochet in single crochet, and repeat from * around. Cut red. Join another strand of orange.

16. Round 13: With 2 orange strands, chain 3, double crochet in each double crochet around. Cut 1 strand of orange. Join 1 strand of yellow.

17. Round 14: With orange and yellow strands, chain 3, double crochet in each double crochet around.

18. Fasten off and weave loose ends.

Ribbed Cabled Knit Hat Pattern

Materials

- 1 skein of Lion Brand Wool-Ease Chunky or any other bulky weight yarn
- 1 set of 16' circular needles in size 10 ½
- 1 set of 5 double-pointed needles in size 10 ½
- Stitch markers
- Cable needle
- Yarn needle

Instructions

1. Using your circular needles and a longtail cast-on, CO 72 stitches and join to knit in the round.
2. K1, P1 Repeat to end of first round and PM.
3. Continue in K1, P1 ribbing until your piece measures four inches long.
4. Round 1: P2, K6 (for cable), P2, K2, P1, K2, P1, K2, PM
5. Repeat this pattern three more times, placing a second marker at the beginning of your second round, so you know where the next round begins.
6. Round 2: Same as Round 1.
7. Round 3: P2, SL 3 sts onto the cable needle and place it behind your work. K the next 3 sts, then K the 3 sts from the cable needle back onto your circular needle. P2, K2, P1, K2, P1, K2, SM. Repeat this pattern three more times to complete Round 3.
8. Repeat Round 1 for 5 rounds, repeating round 3 in the next round.
9. Continue this pattern until your hat measures 8'.
10. To begin decreasing, P2, K2, K2TOG, K2, P2, K2TOG, P1, K2TOG, P1, K2TOG, SM.
11. Continue the pattern 3 more times for the rest of this round.
12. Onto a DPN, P2, K5, P2, K1, P1, K1, P1, K1.Continue in the pattern to the end of the round so you have 14 sts each on 4 dpns.
13. Next Round: P2TOG, K2TOG, K1, K2TOG, P2TOG, K1, P1, K1, P1, K1. Repeat this pattern 3 more times until you have 10 sts on each needle.
14. P1, K3, P1, K1, P1, K1, P1, K1, repeating this pattern for the rest of the round.
15. K2TOG for the entire round, leaving a total of 5 sts on each of the 4 dpns.

16. K2TOG for another round, slipping the last st on Needles 1 and 3 to the next needle and leaving a total of ten stitches. Cut the yarn, leaving 6–8 inches of yarn, and thread it through a yarn needle. Slip the sts off the dpns and onto the yarn needle, running the yarn needle through the last ten sts and pulling it tight. Weave in all the ends and fold up the brim.

Sun Hat With a Ribbon

Materials

- 1 ball medium worsted-weight yarn (pink)
- 1 ball medium worsted-weight yarn (grey)
- J 10/6mm crochet hook

Gauge

- 13 single crochet makes 4''
- 14 rows make 4''

Instructions

1. Crochet the striped round top part of the hat with pink and grey yarn alternately in circles.
2. Note: the stripes should be 2 rows wide. Make a slip stitch at the end of each row to join the ends. Start new rows and win a chain [chain 1 for single crochets and chain 2 for double crochet).
3. With grey yarn, make 3 chains. Slip stitch to join in a ring.
4. Row 1: single crochet 6 in the ring, slip stitch at the end.
5. Row 2: chain 1, single crochets 2 in each stitch for 6 stitches around the row, slip stitch.
6. Row 3: attach the pink yarn. Chain 1, [single crochet, 2sc] repeat [ ] 6 times around the row, slip stitch at the end.
7. Row 4: chain 1, [single crochet 2, 2 single crochet] repeat [ ] 6 times around the row, slip stitch at the end.
8. Row 5: chain 1, [single crochet 3, 2 single crochet] repeat [ ] 6 times around the row, slip stitch. Total = 30 stitches after completing this row.
9. Row 6: chain 1, [single crochet 4, 2 single crochet] repeat [ ] 6 times around the row, slip stitch. Total = 36 stitches after completing this row.
10. Row 7: Chain 1, [single crochet 5, 2 single crochet] Repeat [ ] 6 times around the row, slip stitch. Total = 42 stitches after completing this row.
11. Row 8: Chain 1, [single crochet 6, 2 single crochet] Repeat [ ] 6 times around the row,

slip stitch. Total = 48 stitches after completing this row.

12. Row 9: Chain 1, [single crochet 7, 2 single crochet] Repeat [ ] 6 times around the row, slip stitch. Total = 54 stitches after completing this row.

13. Row 10: Chain 1, [single crochet 8, 2 single crochet] Repeat [ ] 6 times around the row, slip stitch. Total = 60 stitches after completing this row.

14. Row 11: Chain 1, [single crochet 19, 2SC] Repeat [ ] 3 times around the row, slip stitch. Total = 63 stitches

15. Row 12: Chain 1, [single crochet 9, 2SC] Repeat [ ] 6 times around the row, slip stitch. Total = 66 stitches.

16. Crochet the side mesh of the hat using the grey yarn.

17. Row 13: Chain 3 [double crochet in the second stitch (skip one stitch), Chain 1] Repeat [ ] all along the row. Join with a slip stitch and start the next row

18. Row 14: Chain 3, [double crochet in the second stitch (skip one stitch), Chain 1]. Repeat [ ] all around the row. Make sure you are making the double crochet in the current row on top of a double crochet from the previous row.

19. Continue Row 14 the same as you did for Row 13: [double crochet in the second stitch, Chain 1]

20. Make every double crochet stitch in Row 14 on top of the double crochet stitch of the previous row.

21. Make 4 more rows like Rows 13 and 14

22. Make a line imitating the ribbon to be attached using the pink yarn.

23. Row 1: Chain 1 and single crochet in every single crochet around the row, finish with a slip stitch.

24. Row 2: Attach the pink yarn, Chain 1, single crochet in every single crochet around the row, slip stitch.

25. Rows 3–4: Repeat Row 2 with the pink yarn.

26. Row 5: Switch to grey yarn: Repeat Row 1.

27. Make the finishing rows using grey yarn.

28. Row 6: Chain 1, [single crochet 2, 2 single crochet]. Repeat [ ] all around the row, slip stitch at the end.

29. Row 7: Chain 1, [single crochet 3, 2 single crochet]. Repeat [ ] all around the row, and finish with a slip stitch. Cut off the yarn, make a knot, and weave in the end.

Blue Beret Hat Pattern

Materials

- 1 ball Lion Wool
- 4 & 8 DPNS

Gauge

- (Taken in the round, in the pattern) body = 4st/inch
- Ribbing = 5st/inch un-stretched

Instructions

1. Cast on 72 with size 4 needles
2. Work k1p1 around for 1.5 inches
3. Next row, k2m1 repeat for row
4. Switch to size 8 needles
5. K8p1 repeat for row
6. Work till the full length of the hat is: 8.5 inches for tam; 7 inches for toque
7. K2together 4 times, p1 repeat for row
8. K2together 2 times, p1 repeat for row
9. K2together, p1 repeat for row
10. Cut a long tail, and thread it through the remaining stitches 3 times, weave the end inside the hat
11. Weave in the cast on the tail.
12. For the toque, make a two-inch pompom, trim, and fasten.

Flower Baby Hat Knitting Pattern

Materials

- 80 yards of worsted weight yarn (#4)
- 8 yards of DK or worsted for flower
- 4 yards of DK or worsted for leaves
- Size 7 double-pointed needles

Gauge

- 5 stitches = 1 inch on size 7

Instructions

Instructions are given for newborns, with 3–6 months and 6–12 months in parentheses.

1. Cast on 60 (70, 80) stitches. Knit around and attach yarn to the beginning stitch to close up the gap.
2. Continue knitting every round until the piece measures 5.5' (6.5', 7.5'). NOTE: If you want the brim to roll more, keep knitting for another inch.
3. To work the crown, do the decrease rows as follows: -Round 1: Knit 8 st, K2TOG; repeat until the end of the round 54 (63, 72) sts remaining.
4. Round 2 and all even-numbered rounds: K.
5. Round 3: Knit 7 st, K2TOG; repeat until the end of the round 48 (56, 64) sts remaining.
6. Round 5: Knit 6 st, K2TOG; repeat until the end of the round 42 (49, 56) sts remaining.
7. Round 7: Knit 5 st, K2TOG; repeat until the end of the round 36 (42, 48) sts remaining.
8. Round 9: Knit 4 st, K2TOG; repeat until the end of the round 30 (35, 40) sts remaining.
9. Round 11: Knit 3 st, K2TOG; repeat until the end of the round 24 (28, 32) sts remaining.
10. Round 13: Knit 2 st, K2TOG; repeat until the end of the round 18 (21, 24) sts remaining.
11. Round 15: Knit 1 st, K2TOG; repeat until the end of the round 12 (14, 16) sts remaining.
12. Round 17: K2TOG; repeat until the end of round 6 (7, 8) sts remaining.
13. After Round 17, cut yarn, leaving a 6-inch tail. Thread the tail onto a darning needle and then weave the needle through the remaining stitches. Slide them off the needles and pull like a drawstring to close up the hole. Weave in the remainder of the tail.

Rose:

The rose is worked in one long strip and then rolled up. You'll start by making 4 small petals, and then 3 medium-sized petals, and 3 large petals, and they are all connected. It looks like a lot of instructions, but this is easy knitting that works up very fast.

1. Cast on 5 st.
2. Row 1: K1 f&b, K4—6 sts total.
3. Row 2: P4, P1 f&b, P1—7 sts total.
4. Row 3: K7.
5. Row 4: P7.
6. Row 5: K1, k2tog, K4—6 sts.
7. Row 6: P3, p2tog, P1—5 sts total.
8. Repeat Rows 1–6 three more times, so you'll end with 4 petals.
9. Now, you are going to proceed to knit the medium petals on the same strip, so don't cut your yarn; just keep knitting.
10. Row 7: K1 f&b, K4—6 sts total.
11. Row 8: P4, P1 f&b, P1—7 sts total.
12. Row 9: K1 f&b, K6—8 sts total.
13. Row 10: P6, P1 f&b, P1—9 sts total.
14. Rows 11 and 13: K9.
15. Rows 12 and 14: P9.
16. Rows 15 and 17: K1, k2tog, K to end.
17. Rows 16 and 18: P to last 3 sts; p2tog, P1.You should have 5 sts remaining at end of Row 18.
18. Repeats Rows 7–18 two more times, so you've added 3 petals to the strip.
19. Next, you'll knit the large petals on the same strip, without cutting your yarn.
20. Rows, 19, 21, and 23: K1 f&b, K to end.
21. Rows 20, 22, and 24: P to last 2 sts; P1 f&b, P1. At end of Row 24, you should have 11 sts.
22. Rows 25, 27, and 29: K11.
23. Rows 26, 28, and 30: P11.
24. Rows 31, 33, and 35: K1, k2tog, K to end.
25. Rows 32, 34, and 36: P to last 3 sts; p2tog, P1. At end of Row 36, you should have 5

sts.

26. Repeat Rows 19–36 two more times.
27. Row 37: K1, k2tog, K2—4 sts remaining.
28. Row 38: P1, p2tog, P1—3 sts.
29. Row 39: K1, k2tog—2 sts.
30. Row 40: p2tog. Cut the tail and slip through the last stitch. Tighten the strand to secure the knot.
31. -Press the petal strip. Starting from the small petal end, roll up the strip with the wrong side facing outwards. Stitch the bottom edges together, so your rose does not unwind. Curl the petals outward.

Leaf:

1. You will make two leaves—a small and a big one.
2. For the large leaf, cast on 3 st.
3. Row 1 and all odd-numbered (Wrong Side) rows: P.
4. Row 2 (RS): [K1 f&b] twice, K1—5 sts total.
5. Row 4: [K1 f&b] twice, K3—7 sts total.
6. Row 6: [K1 f&b] twice, K5—9 sts total.
7. Row 8: [K1 f&b] twice, K7—11 sts total.
8. Row 10: [K1 f&b] twice, K9—13 sts total.
9. Row 12: K.
10. Row 14: SSK, K9, k2tog—11 sts total.
11. Row 16: SSK, K7, k2tog—9 sts total.
12. Row 18: SSK, K5, k2tog—7 sts total.
13. Row 20: SSK, K3, k2tog—5 sts total.
14. Row 22: SSK, K1, k2tog—3 sts total.
15. Row 24: Sl2, PSSO—1 st.
16. Cut the tail and slip through the last stitch. Tighten the strand to secure the knot.
17. For the small leaf, follow the same pattern, for Rows 1–7, omit Rows 8–15, and finish with Rows 16–24.
18. Attach one tip of each leaf to the stitched base of the flower. Before attaching the flower to the hat, be sure to roll up the brim so that it is placed where it will be seen, and not inside the brim!

Sunflower Hat

Materials

- Red Heart Super Saver in Coffee (A), Gold (B), Aran (C), and Paddy Green (D)
- 1 US I/9 (5.50 mm) crochet hook
- 1 US K/10 ½ (6.50 mm) crochet hook
- 1 tapestry needle.

Instructions

Special stitches: fpsc (front post single crochet) insert the hook from the front to the back of the post of the stitch and back out to the right side, yarn over, and pull through both loops on the hook.

Flower:

1. With Color A and a size I/9 crochet hook, create a magic circle and ch3, 9dc into the circle and join.
2. Round 1: ch3, dc into same st, 2dc into each st around, ch1* join in 3rd starting ch
3. Round 3: Join Color B in any ch3 sp, *ch3, sc into ch1 sp* around, join
4. Round 4, sl st into ch3 sp ch1, *(sc, hdc, dc, trb, dc, hdc sc)* into each ch3 sp around, join into ch1

Hat:

5. Round 1: With the wrong side of the flower facing you and a size J/10 ½ crochet hook attach Color A around any dc post, ch1 *fpsc, ch1* around join in ch1 sp
6. Round 2: ch1, 2sc into ch1 sp around, join, turn
7. Round 3: Join Color C in any sc, ch1, 1sc in each st around and join in ch1
8. Round 4: ch3 *hdc, ch1, sk 1 st* repeat around and join in 2nd ch
9. Round 5: sl st into ch1 sp, ch3 *hdc into ch1 sp, ch1* repeat around and join in 2nd ch
10. Round 6–9: Repeat Row 5, fasten off Color C at end of Round 9
11. Row 10: Join Color A in any ch1 sp, ch2, *hdc into hdc st, hdc into ch1 sp* repeat around and join in 2nd ch, fasten off Color A

12. Row 11: Join Color B in any hdc st, ch2, hdc in each st around, join in 2nd ch

13. Row 12: ch1, sc in each st around, join, fasten off and weave in ends of the large leaf.

14. With color D and size I/9 crochet hook ch6, in 2nd ch from hook sc, hdc, dc, hdc, sc in the next sts, 2sc into end st, hdc, dc hdc, sc into the back of the chain, fasten off, leave a long tail to attach to the hat the small leaf.

15. With color D and size I/9 crochet hook ch5, in 2nd ch from hook, sc, hdc, dc, hdc, sc into same st as hdc, fasten off and leave a long tail to attach to hat.

16. Attach both leaves under the petals of the sunflower, pull the tails to the back, tie them together and weave in a spiral.

17. With color D and size I/9 crochet hook, attach yarn to dc post next to leaves. Ch 20, in 2nd ch from hook, sc to end of ch, sl st around joining post and ch20, 2nd ch from hook sc, sc to end of ch. Twist the chains tightly and let go. (They will stay twisted. If not twist again.)

CONCLUSION

Thank you for reading this book. One of the good things about learning to crochet is that you can start making unique gifts for the people you care about, and you can even start selling your creations if you want to. Your own style will shine through in every crocheted creation. You can even make some fun, unique accessories for your home. Nothing compares to the satisfaction of putting your heart and soul into a project and then watching as people express their appreciation for it.

If you're willing to look, you'll find a fantastic group of crocheters that are quite active in various internet communities. Seeing what other crocheters are up to on online discussion groups is a terrific way to pick up new ideas and techniques. If you want to learn how to crochet like a pro, it's no different from learning any other talent. If you put in the time and effort, you can master any skill.

You can choose from a wide variety of starter projects if you're just getting started. And if you're still unsure, refer to the handy reference section I included in this book. However, you shouldn't start with the more complicated patterns. Learn the basic ones at your own pace. The more you use it, the more you'll understand it, and soon you'll be able to wrap up tasks in a single day. Gradually, you'll reach a point when you're creating your own patterns from scratch.

Assuming you've already tried your hand at several simple crochet projects and mastered the fundamentals, the next step is to take your practice to the next level. Make your friends and family holiday gifts of one-of-a-kind scarves, headbands, and pouch bags, or try something more advanced like curtains or tablecloths. I don't doubt that they will treasure and appreciate these creations just as much as you do.

Never feel constrained by this book's patterns. Try to find even more complex structures. Experiment with different color schemes. Make use of any fine cord of twisted fibers or crochet threads you can get your hands on. Strengthen your abilities and create novel approaches and routines. A complicated crochet project shouldn't scare you.

I hope you find the information you need to get started with this book, and I don't doubt that after a week you will have mastered all the fundamental stitches and more. How quickly you learn to crochet like a pro depends on how much time and effort you put into it. When you reach that level of proficiency, nothing but the stars will be able to hold you back.

Happy crocheting!

Made in the USA
Monee, IL
12 December 2023

49019987R00052